"I have an insatiable hunge devotionals that draw me closer the Father's heart, revealing more of His character and nature. Jill Higgins' *Grateful for God, A through Z* does just that. Letter by letter, she invites the reader to pause, behold the beauty of creation, and lift our eyes and hearts in praise and worship to our Creator. This will be one of the devotionals I go back to again and again."

—Melannie Jackson
Executive Pastor,
New Life Church, Port Townsend, Washington

"My messy and meandering process of growing closer to Jesus has always been punctuated with guidance and inspiration from others who are making their way, maybe imperfectly, toward the same goal. In this short devotional you'll find, as I have, creative and accessible thoughts from a genuine follower of Christ. Jill's humility and insight make each entry a joyful invitation into many attributes of God you have likely not yet explored. Prepare for 26 days of adventure; journey forward with Jill!"

—Nate Swanson
Lead Pastor, New City Church, Great Falls, Montana

"Pastoring university students for the past 26 years, I've always wanted students to know God intimately and to see the many ways He reveals Himself to us. Jill Higgins' book *Grateful for God, A through Z*, beautifully shares what intimacy with God can look like when we are open to revelation and vulnerable to God. I recommend this devotional to you as a refreshing reminder of who God is."

—Tim Kern
Director of Chi Alpha Campus Ministries,
South Bend, Indiana

"I have been in missions and ministry for over 15 years, training young people for short term missions cross culturally. In our trainings, the goal is for students to share the gospel out of the knowledge of God so it is flowing from an intimate relationship with Him. As I read Jill's book, I cannot help but to think how her writing (and experience) demonstrates so beautiful what we try to teach every day! Through her sharing, you can see how God has touched her heart, spoken His word to her and that translated to her living a missional life sharing His goodness with others. It is such an encouragement to read a book that is coming from an overflow of His word in someone's life. Thank you, Jill!"

—Samantha Krebs
Co-founder Asian Xpressions, Kansas City, Missouri

"In my nearly 40 years of pastoral and educational ministry, I always appreciate finding new resources that inspire my life of faith. Jill Higgins' *Grateful for God, A through Z* has found a home in my soul. Her everyday look at many of the characteristics of God truly show us the love and goodness of our Heavenly Father. I commend this read to you as I trust it will nourish your soul as well and to God be the glory."

—Rev. Stuart A. Smith
President, Hollow Rock camp meeting association, Toronto, Ohio and Retired Campus Chaplain, Asbury University, Wilmore, Kentucky.

GRATEFUL
FOR
GOD
A THROUGH Z

26 DAYS OF HIS CHARACTER

JILL HIGGINS

ILLUSTRATED BY
MEGAN CORDEIRO

CLAY BRIDGES
PRESS

Grateful for God A through Z
26 Days of His Character

Copyright © 2023 by Jill Higgins
Illustrated by Megan Cordeiro

Published by Lucid Books in Houston, TX
www.LucidBooks.com

Unless otherwise marked Scripture quotations are taken from the Holy Bible, New International Version®, NIV®. Copyright ©1973, 1978, 1984, 2011 by Biblica, Inc.™ (NIV) Used by permission of Zondervan. All rights reserved worldwide. www.zondervan.com The "NIV" and "New International Version" are trademarks registered in the United States Patent and Trademark Office by Biblica, Inc.™

Scripture quotations marked (ESV) are taken from the ESV® Bible (The Holy Bible, English Standard Version®), copyright © 2001 by Crossway, a publishing ministry of Good News Publishers. Used by permission. All rights reserved.

Scripture quotations marked (KJV) are taken from the King James Version (KJV): King James Version, public domain.

Scripture quotations marked (NASB) are taken from the (NASB®) New American Standard Bible®, Copyright © 1960, 1971, 1977, 1995, 2020 by The Lockman Foundation. Used by permission. All rights reserved. http://www.lockman.org

Scripture quotations marked (NLT) are taken from the Holy Bible, New Living Translation, copyright ©1996, 2004, 2015 by Tyndale House Foundation. Used by permission of Tyndale House Publishers, Carol Stream, Illinois 60188. All rights reserved.

Scripture quotations marked (TPT) are from The Passion Translation®. Copyright © 2017, 2018, 2020 by Passion & Fire Ministries, Inc. Used by permission. All rights reserved. ThePassionTranslation.com.

Scripture quotations marked (AMP) are taken from the Amplified Bible. Copyright © 1954, 1958, 1962, 1964, 1965, 1987 by The Lockman Foundation, La Habra, CA. All rights reserved. Used by Permission.

ISBN: 978-1-68488-095-9
eISBN: 978-1-68488-097-3

Special Sales: Most Lucid Books titles are available in special quantity discounts. Custom imprinting or excerpting can also be done to fit special needs. Contact Lucid Books at Info@LucidBooks.com

To my son, Mekai Rhys

I am proud of the man you are becoming. Your love for Jesus is evident in everything you do and say. You bring me so much joy through your daily worship and weekly live shows as Recap Pastor Mekai.

Don't let anyone look down on you because you are young, but set an example for the believers in speech, in conduct, in love, in faith and in purity.

—1 Tim. 4:12

Table of Contents

Introduction

Ever since I was a child, I have found myself spending many hours alone in nature. I didn't really understand why I was drawn to the outdoors at the time, but I now recognize it was a connection with God's creation. Today, I go into nature and feel unified with God.

During my time outdoors, I connect with God through all my senses. Although I can interact with Him this way, I struggle to know Him . . . really know Him. I grew up in church, so I have a vast amount of knowledge about God, but I never got to know Him intimately. I did all the religious activities I was taught in an effort to seek Him on a deeper level. I did things such as read the Bible, pray, serve my church and community, and listen to worship music; however, a hole remained in my heart.

A couple of years ago, I went on a weekend spiritual retreat by myself in the woods. I was in a season where I desperately needed to connect with God. While there, I saw and experienced Him, unlike any other time. A few months later, my best friend, Megan, sent me back outside to search for ways God loved me in His creation. While God and I spent quality time together, He showed me many of His characteristics and how he loved me. Shortly after that, my church did a 21-day fast. During that time, it finally clicked for me.

All my life I knew most of the titles, names, and characteristics of God. Sadly, I only identified with Him as someone who performed in a moment of need. For example, I thought He utilized His quality as Healer when I was sick or in pain. The truth is that these attributes of God are who He is all the time. He doesn't just heal when I am hurt; He is God the Healer. He heals me all the time to repair my brokenness. Simultaneously, He comforts me as my Comforter. At the same time, He extends His peace because He is my Prince of Peace and guides me as my Counselor. He is all these things and more all the time due to my ongoing, continuous need for them.

I dabbled in writing a year prior to my retreat. Those short works spoke of lessons He taught me during that season. I shared them with a few friends and family. It was during Thanksgiving after the fast that Megan approached me about writing a daily devotional for the month. It was then that the Holy Spirit revealed Himself to me and inspired me to write 26 characteristics of God. I am grateful for that time.

My greatest desire is that through these devotionals, you will encounter Him similarly and draw closer to Him in a deeper relationship.

Jill

Author and Funisher

A – Author

Looking unto Jesus the author and finisher of our faith; who for the joy that was set before him endured the cross, despising the shame, and is set down at the right hand of the throne of God.

—Heb. 12:2 KJV

The Lord Almighty has sworn, "Surely, as I have planned, so it will be, and as I have purposed, so it will happen."

—Isa. 14:24

"For I know the plans I have for you," says the Lord. "They are plans for good and not for disaster, to give you a future and a hope."

—Jer. 29:11 NLT

I enjoy reading. I'm not usually a fan of books that give you the ending up front and then jump back to tell the story. Yet the greatest story ever told does exactly that. In God's mercy story, our salvation story, we win in the end.

I marvel at God's creativity and the complexity of His story, and yet it is so simple—believe and confess as well as surrender and obey. God's story began well before He created the world. When He formed the earth, He had already chosen you and me and penned us into His story—a story layered with His sovereign will and our free will. His perfect plot established all things without fault. But wait! There's a plot twist. He gave us literary freedom to edit our own story. Sadly, we did, and it created an eternity with death and separated us from God.

Every great story has an adversary, and ours is no different. Death came to steal, kill, and destroy the story God wrote. Death is not a very good writer, although he does have the ability to mess up a good narrative. Death is not creative either. He just takes a good tale and spins it to appear bad, taking truth and substituting a few words to make a lie. What he failed to realize, however, is that our Author knows His tale inside and out. Moreover, God recognizes every incorrect word and rewrites the story to make it even better.

Death, also known as Satan, attempted to write a new ending to each of our stories; however, God gets the final approval of your story and mine. God established the most wonderful turning point. In His mercy and grace, He chose you! He sent His Son to permanently change the narrative by taking on Death and defeating him handily on the cross and in His resurrection. When we accept Jesus as our Savior, we accept the new ending to our story—life.

Here's one last twist to the book. The end is really the beginning. Stay tuned for the sequel. I am extremely grateful to and humbled by God, my Author, for changing the end of my story.

Recommended worship:
"Mercy Story" by Futures

LOVE
Closet
each
DEVO
w/ a SONG

7

B – Beautiful

For since the creation of the world God's invisible qualities—his eternal power and divine nature—have been clearly seen, being understood from what has been made, so that people are without excuse.

—Rom. 1:20

You formed my innermost being, shaping my delicate inside and my intricate outside, and wove them all together in my mother's womb. I thank you, God, for making me so mysteriously complex! Everything you do is marvelously breathtaking. It simply amazes me to think about it! How thoroughly you know me, Lord!

—Ps. 139:13–14 TPT

*B*eautiful is not a word I have ever used to describe God. In fact, I rarely use the word to describe anyone, especially not me. Until recently, the word *beautiful* was reserved solely for nature. I have had a shift in perspective.

My best friend and I give each other homework as it relates to our current spiritual journeys. I love nature and spend a lot of time with God there. The homework she gave me was to go into nature to write down what nature tells me about the character of God. I was to ponder how nature models the relationship I want with Him. Of course, I was struck by the beauty of it all as I always am, but for the first time, God revealed Himself as Beautiful.

We are the only beings of God's workmanship that He created in His image. Many of the Bible teachings I have heard put the focus on His emotional and mindful attributes. They focus on things such as the fruits of the Spirit—love, joy, patience—and having a mind like Christ—taking thoughts captive and thinking on those things that are pure, noble, trustworthy, and more. I had never considered beauty as an aspect of God.

Romans tells us that God placed His qualities in His creation. I see beauty all around me. Every tree showcases creation's beauty. During the fall season, the trees say by their dance, "Look at me." The leaves win the beauty pageant in nature. The mountains demonstrate perfection and intentionality in each curve as they stand magnificently in all their splendor. The water, gentle yet powerful, quietly speaks in a soft whisper as it flows over the rocks. The birds and squirrels radiate joy and playfulness as they go from branch to branch.

As I watched and heard God reveal Himself as beautiful to me, He brought to my mind Psalm 139:13–14. He tells me by His mind (He purposely thought out every detail), soul (with great love, joy, and passion), and body (by His hands He formed me, and by His breath He gives me life) that I was fashioned beautifully inside and out, magnificently complex, and marvelously breathtaking.

I am grateful for the God of Beauty who created me in His image. *Beautiful* is a new word in my vocabulary that defines who I am. I pray that you, too, can proudly and confidently say, "Because I am made in His image, I am beautiful."

Recommended worship:
"Beautiful Saviour" by Planetshakers

C – Comforter

Praise be to the God and Father of our Lord Jesus Christ, the Father of compassion and the God of all comfort, who comforts us in all our troubles, so that we can comfort those in any trouble with the comfort we ourselves receive from God.

—2 Cor. 1:3–4

As a mother comforts her child, so will I comfort you.

—Isa. 66:13

Those who live in the shelter of the Most High will find rest in the shadow of the Almighty. This I declare about the Lord: He alone is my refuge, my place of safety; he is my God, and I trust him. He will cover you with his feathers. He will shelter you with his wings. His faithful promises are your armor and protection. The Lord says, "I will rescue those who love me. I will protect those who trust in my name. When they call on me, I will answer; I will be with them in trouble. I will rescue and honor them."

—Ps. 91:1–2, 4, 14–15 NLT

W ho's the person that comes to mind when you need comforting? Your mom? Spouse? Friend? What draws you to the person you identified?

My mom was always the one I went to for comfort as a child and young adult. Trust is what drew me to her. My mom is a great, godly woman, yet she is flawed, imperfect, and not always able to provide the comfort I need. There is only one who is perfect in every way and can supply all our needs—God the Father, Jesus, and the Holy Spirit.

I thought comforting was reserved for seasons of pain such as a loss of a family member or friend, relationship problems, or job-related stresses. Gosh, was I wrong! A recent season took me on a spiritual journey of healing past brokenness; breaking me of known and unknown sins; teaching me humility, forgiveness, and faith; and receiving grace. During that time, there were many occasions for which I needed consoling. In times when I felt shame, fear, disappointment, hopelessness, embarrassment, and sadness, I ran to God and jumped right under the shelter of His wings. He is the only one who truly is capable of comforting me in all these situations.

What I also discovered in a lesson that is still fresh today is that trust and vulnerability are requisite to comforting. We are at our most vulnerable state when we need comforting. Consequently, the person we go to is a trusted friend or family member. But God really is the only one to do this perfectly. He is trustworthy in telling me what I need to hear, holding me accountable, encouraging me, and loving me regardless of what I disclose. Therefore, I am able to be vulnerable and tell

Him everything I think and feel. What is the result of that? I am at peace.

I'm not dismissing the advantage of having a trusted friend, spouse, or family member to provide you comfort. God placed these people in our lives to walk alongside us in our pain and suffering, as well as in our joy and happiness. However, I have learned that it is best to go to God first and then follow up with a spiritual friend or family member. When I do this in reverse, it usually takes longer to get the peace I'm seeking.

I am grateful for Jehovah Nacham, God my Comforter. He willingly waits for me to come and welcomes me with open arms. I nestle up under the shelter of His wings, getting in a position of stillness at which point He pours out His love and gives me peace.

Recommended worship:
"Still/PEACE" by Hillsong Worship

14

D – Door

So Jesus again said to them, "Truly, truly, I say to you, I am the door of the sheep. I am the door. If anyone enters by me, he will be saved and will go in and out and find pasture."

—John 10:7, 9 ESV

Jesus answered, "I am the way and the truth and the Life. No one comes to the Father except through me."

—John 14:6

"Look! I stand at the door and knock. If you hear my voice and open the door, I will come in, and we will share a meal together as friends."

—Rev. 3:20 NLT

In the Gospel of John, Jesus makes seven "I Am" statements. The third one is in our verse above—"I am the door." In this one verse, Jesus makes three bold proclamations. First, this man who many believed was just a prophet stated, "I AM," the name God called Himself to Moses. Jesus states, "I am God." Second, Jesus uses the word *the*. He is emphasizing that He is *the* door, not *a* door. The world tells us there are multiple ways to get to heaven or euphoria. They say to "just be a good person," "just be spiritual," or "there are different gods for different purposes." Jesus says that there is only one way, and it is Him. Then He states that He is the "door." A door gives us access to and from something. In this case, Jesus is saying, "I am the only access to God the Father." He follows this up a few chapters later when He says that He is the Way—Jesus is the only way to God and heaven.

In Revelation, we see Jesus is standing at the door knocking. If He is the door, which door is He knocking on? He stands and knocks on the door to our hearts. He is the only door to God, but once we get in at salvation, He needs to transform our hearts to be like His as He works to heal and sanctify us. We read in Proverbs that everything flows from the heart. Our heart is the house of all our sins and bondages. Jesus is saying, "If you let me in, I can give you healing, forgiveness, freedom from addictions, surrender, faith, trust, and so much more such as love, peace, kindness, patience, and self-control." When we open the door to our heart and allow Him to enter, transformation happens. We are restored, renewed, and released from bondage. That is something to celebrate. Will you open your door and welcome Him in as He did for you?

I am grateful that Jesus is THE DOOR. He doesn't complicate it. His way is simple—love me, love others. Welcome, Jesus. Come in, and have a seat. Make yourself at home. Be the change in me. We have eternity to get to know each other.

Recommended worship:
"The Change in Me" by Casting Crowns

E – Empty

Have this mind among yourselves, which is yours in Christ Jesus, who, though he was in the form of God, did not count equality with God a thing to be grasped, but emptied himself, by taking the form of a servant, being born in the likeness of men.

—Phil. 2:5–7 ESV

The behavior of the self-life is obvious: Sexual immorality, lustful thoughts, pornography, chasing after things instead of God, manipulating others, hatred of those who get in your way, senseless arguments, resentment when others are favored, temper tantrums, angry quarrels, only thinking of yourself, being in love with your own opinions, being envious of the blessings of others, murder, uncontrolled addictions, wild parties, and all other similar behavior . . . . But the fruit produced by the Holy Spirit within you is divine love in all its varied expressions: joy that overflows, peace that subdues, patience that endures, kindness in action, a life full of virtue, faith that prevails, gentleness of heart, and strength of spirit.

—Gal. 5:19–23 TPT

The God we serve is one of a kind in so many ways. How He stands out among all the other so-called gods is His humility. The same God—Jesus—who created the universe and everything in it humbled Himself by becoming a human, dying for our sins, and rising again to reign for eternity. In the verses above, it says He emptied Himself. That does not mean He gave up His divinity; He was still God. What it means is that He gave up heaven's glory (a beauty manifested in perfection) to live on earth in all our mess. He took on human nature, which required food, shelter, and rest. He limited His ability to be all-knowing, all-present, and all-powerful. The King of kings became a servant to all.

As Christians, we are commanded to live like Jesus; therefore, we are to humble ourselves and empty our hearts. Unlike Christ, however, we are filled with all kinds of ugly. Galatians 5 lists many of those things, and it is not an all-inclusive list. We need to empty ourselves of anything that goes against the will of God—things such as expectations, pride, insecurities, our own will, anxiety, fear, relationships, work that takes priority over God, unforgiveness, and more.

What an awesome God we serve! When we empty ourselves of all these things, it creates space for Him to fill us up. He gives gifts of love, joy, peace, and all good things. He also replaces unforgiveness with the ability to forgive and extend grace. He exchanges anxiousness and fear with peace and courage; He anoints our relationships and gives us a multitude of blessings.

Recommended worship:
"Fill Me" by River Valley Worship

F – Forgiver

If we confess our sins, he is faithful and just and will forgive us our sins and purify us from all unrighteouness.

—1 John 1:9

For if you forgive other people when they sin against you, your heavenly Father will also forgive you. But if you do not forgive others their sins, your Father will not forgive your sins.

—Matt. 6:14–15

Then Peter came to Jesus and asked, "Lord, how many times shall I forgive my brother or sister who sins against me? Up to seven times?" Jesus answered, "I tell you, not seven times, but seventy-seven times."

—Matt. 18:21–22

God is a forgiver of sins. No matter what we do, God will forgive our sins and remember them no more. This is made possible because of the power of the cross. When Jesus took our sins upon Himself on the cross, we acquired free access to God who graciously forgave us. We just have to confess our sin(s) and repent.

One of my favorite people in the Bible is David. Of all the Bible characters, this guy's sins were exposed. He had an adulterous affair, he murdered, he lied, and he did not hold his son accountable after he raped his sister. And who knows what else David did that we never heard about? But God calls him a man after His own heart because David had a repentant heart. Once his sin was exposed, David quickly confessed it and repented to God who lovingly responded with grace. Jesus's blood covered all our sins all at once, and we never have to feel shame or fear again because of them. However, each time we sin (because we will continue to do so in this world), we are to confess again. We do that because a repentant heart encourages us to remain within God's will.

We often hear it said that we should forgive because forgiveness helps the forgiver heal and move on. While there may be truth to the statement that healing comes from forgiving, that is not the reason we are to forgive. We forgive because God commands us to. He is justified in commanding us because He forgives us freely, without condition. In fact, while we were still sinners, purposefully going against His will, He sent Jesus to die for us, thus making a way for our sins to be forgiven permanently every single time (Rom. 5:8).

God forgives us, and therefore commands us to forgive others. But there is a second part to this command mentioned several chapters later in Matthew. Although Jesus's blood covered all our sins instantly, making our spirits right with

God, He expects us to seek His forgiveness each time we sin and acknowledge those areas we haven't fully surrendered to Him. Because we are to be like Him, we are commanded to forgive our family members, our friends, and our enemies every single time. And because Christ died for us while we were still sinners, we are told to die to self and forgive our transgressors even when they do not ask for or seek our forgiveness. Wow! That is so hard to do. But remember that earlier we said, "We should forgive because forgiveness helps the forgiver heal and move on." Isn't God a great and awesome God who gives us strength to do the unthinkable and rewards us for it? I'm so grateful for my God, the Forgiver.

Recommended worship:
"The Power of the Cross" by Casting Crowns

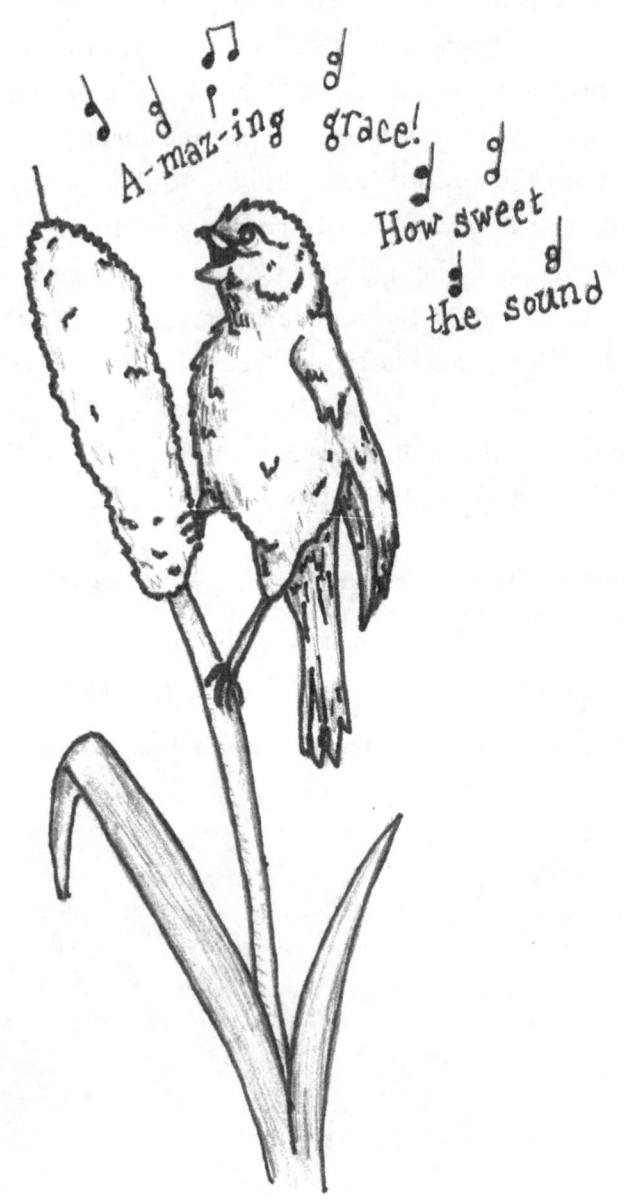

G – Gracious God

For it is by grace you have been saved, <u>through faith</u>—and this is not from yourselves, it <u>is the gift of God</u>— not by works, so that no one can boast.

—Eph. 2:8–9

And if by grace, then it cannot be based on works; if it were, grace would no longer be grace.

—Rom. 11:6

So let us come boldly to the throne of our gracious God. There we will receive his mercy, and we will find grace to help us when we need it most.

—Heb. 4:16 NLT

You may be surprised to know I am horrible with vocabulary. I don't know the definition of many words. Often when I write or talk, a word will pop in my head, but I don't know what it means. If I'm writing, I look up the definition to make sure it's the right word for what I am trying to convey. Many churchy words are like that. I grew

25

up in church and heard many words I did not fully grasp the meaning of. *Grace* was one of those words.

If you look up the word *grace* in the dictionary, you'll find six or seven meanings. The biblical meaning is buried toward the end. There is only one definition that matters, and that's God's definition. In short, God's grace means He gives us what we don't deserve, and He gives it to us freely. He gives us love, mercy, and forgiveness of sins over and over regardless of how many times we stumble into sin. He freely gives us undeserved grace time and time again. We don't earn it in any way; we just receive this gift with gratitude. Is it too good to be true? To the world it is, but to Christians, it is what makes our God so much greater than the others.

I have a hard time receiving a gift. I feel like I have to return the favor or do something to earn it. Consequently, receiving God's grace is a challenge for me. I'm constantly trying to find ways to earn His grace through my performance or work. I find myself spending more time reading the Bible, praying, or listening to worship songs. Although I enjoy spending most of my time alone, sometimes I find myself trying to earn grace by serving others. Don't misunderstand me; none of these things are bad, and we are instructed to do them. But it comes down to the motive of the heart. God's been exposing pride in my heart. He is showing me that even in the areas where I think I'm doing the right thing, my motives are often fueled by pride. Pride tells me I can win God's favor by doing all these things; grace tells me I can't.

I am grateful that I serve a gracious God. Because of who I

am, I don't deserve His love, forgiveness, mercy, or anything else from Him. But because of His great love for me, I am learning to receive His gift of grace.

Recommended worship:
"Grace" by Laura Story

H – Healer

He forgives all my sins and heals all my diseases.

—Ps. 103:3 NLT

He heals the brokenhearted and binds up their wounds.

—Ps. 147:3

*A few days later, when Jesus again entered Capernaum . . .
Some men came, bringing to him a paralyzed man, carried
by four of them. Since they could not get him to Jesus because
of the crowd, they made an opening in the roof above Jesus
by digging through it and then lowered the mat the man was
lying on. When Jesus saw their faith, he said to the paralyzed
man, "Son, your sins are forgiven." Now some teachers of the
law were sitting there, thinking to themselves, "Why does
this fellow talk like that? He's blaspheming! Who can forgive
sins but God alone?" Immediately Jesus knew in his spirit
that this was what they were thinking in their hearts, and he
said to them, "Why are you thinking these things? Which is
easier: to say to this paralyzed man, 'Your sins are forgiven,'
or to say, 'Get up, take your mat and walk'? But I want
you to know that the Son of Man has authority on earth to*

forgive sins." So he said to the man, "I tell you, get up, take your mat and go home." He got up, took his mat and walked out in full view of them all.

—Mark 2:1, 3–12

No one likes to be in pain whether it's physical, mental, emotional, or most certainly spiritual. Each of us has a tolerance level, a threshold of pain we are capable of sustaining before we seek help. Depending on the type and severity of the pain, it could lead to death. The best physician of the mind, soul, and body is Jehovah Rapha, the God who Heals.

God is capable of healing us regardless of what the root cause is. We often seek prayer for those things that are physical, but sadly, we try to handle emotional, mental, and spiritual pain on our own. Frequently we are just treating symptoms and not the actual source of our pain. For example, anger, lack of intimacy, or over-performing are just symptoms of a wound left open. The root could be pride, control, or a lack of trust. Each of these roots is a condition of the heart, and only God can heal you through the transformation of your heart.

Last year, God took me on a journey to heal from my past. In my pride, I believed I did a good job of healing myself. God chuckled and said, "No, my child. Let's do it right." He and I are still working on healing my brokenness and transforming my heart for His glory.

What I've learned so far on my journey and through the examples in Scripture is that healing, whether it's physical, mental, or emotional, is almost always preceded by spiritual healing. God needs to fix our hearts before He works on the other aspects of our pain. There are times when He heals someone physically, mentally, or emotionally first because it will bring them to salvation, but in most cases, He heals the spiritual part of us first. The above two verses from the Psalms echo this. He heals us from our sins and our brokenness and then from diseases and wounds. It is our spiritual healing that will bring the most glory to His name. When we are spiritually made whole, we will be a testimony to who He is and to His power, whether or not He chooses to heal physically, mentally, and emotionally. If we never get what we think is healing in the physical, mental, or emotional realm, we really will not be concerned because we will trust in His ways and in His timing. He will provide for us, so there is no reason to fear.

I am grateful for my God, the Healer. Due to His work in my heart, I am free of shame and guilt. I am saved, and I am being renewed. I am not completely healed, but He has given me hope and life. I have a story for all the great things He has done and continues to do. What about your story? Is it one of healing?

Recommended worship:
"Healer" by Kari Jobe

I – Intimate

O God of my life, I'm lovesick for you in this weary wilderness. I thirst with the deepest longings to love you more, with cravings in my heart that can't be described. Such yearning grips my soul for you, my God! I'm energized every time I enter your heavenly sanctuary to seek more of your power and drink in more of your glory. For your tender mercies mean more to me than life itself. How I love and praise you, God! Daily I will worship you passionately and with all my heart. My arms will wave to you like banners of praise. I overflow with praise when I come before you, for the anointing of your presence satisfies me like nothing else. You are such a rich banquet of pleasure to my soul. I lie awake each night thinking of you and reflecting on how you help me like a father. I sing through the night under your splendor-shadow, offering up to you my songs of delight and joy! With passion I pursue and cling to you. Because I feel your grip on my life, I keep my soul close to your heart.

—Ps. 63:1–8 TPT

As the deer pants [longingly] for the water brooks, so my soul pants [longingly] for You, O God. My soul (my life, my inner self) thirsts for God, for the living God. When will I come and see the face of God?

—Ps. 42:1–2 AMP

A combination of living in a sexualized culture and a childhood influenced by unhealthy touching skewed my understanding of intimacy. I believed I had to avoid all levels and types of intimacy except maybe between a husband and wife since intimacy and sex went hand in hand.

That affected many areas of my life, including how affectionate I was with those close to me and how I loved them. As a child, sometimes what should have been healthy touching led to the unhealthy kind; therefore, all touching was off limits, including hugging, hand-holding, and massages. What I have recently learned is that intimacy among friends and family is a gift from God because He is a God of Intimacy.

When I recommitted my life to Christ, I prayed regularly for a spiritual friend. Faithfully I prayed, begging and pleading with God for someone who would mentor me spiritually. Year after year passed, and finally, after six years, He gave me my best friend, Megan. To say God's ways and timing are perfect is a complete and utter understatement. I have been blessed beyond measure with the gift of friendship Megan and I share because God did not just give me a spiritual mentor, He gave me a sister in Christ, a partner for His kingdom, and a friend I will die for without question. Nevertheless, our relationship did not come without trials and was forged through a lot of fires.

From the beginning, we established our relationship on Christ. I was seeking a spiritual friend and nothing else. But God had other plans. This friendship would ultimately be built on the foundation of Christ with bricks of trust bound together by the mortar of intimacy. Love, grace, affection, patience, and truth decorate our walls. Looking always to the example of Christ, Megan taught me to trust her on many levels. We worked on trust in communication, trust in emotional vulnerability, trust in our touch, trust in our thoughts, and trust in fun activities, to name a few. Sadly, the bricks of trust were unstable, often falling out of place. Something needed to hold the bricks in place, and that something was intimacy.

When I reflect on my relationship with Christ, I see the same house being built. The closer Megan and I became in our relationship, the more in love and intimate I became with Christ and He with me. I know this is currently backward since my relationship with Christ should be the blueprint of all my other relationships. It is something we continue to work on.

Nonetheless, my relationship with God has become more intimate in the way Megan and I communicate with each other. We're more intimate in the way we touch—not sexual in any way but with love and affection through music, prayer, and God's Word. We're intimate in the way we think, feel, and act toward each other, and we're more intimate in the fun activities we share. Once intimacy became part of our relationship, a fire within me began to burn. It is simultaneously painful and exhilarating as I long for more and more of it. Nothing quenches the thirst that comes from a relationship where trust and intimacy are structurally sound.

I am so grateful for an Intimate God. It's a beautiful thing to be in a relationship where intimacy binds us together.

Recommended worship:
"As the Deer" by Shane & Shane and the Worship Initiative; "Psalm 90" by Shane & Shane

J – Just

*He is the Rock, his works are perfect, and all his ways are just.
A faithful God who does no wrong, upright and just is he.*

—Deut. 32:4

*Righteousness and justice are the foundation of your throne;
love and faithfulness go before you.*

—Ps. 89:14

*But let justice roll on like a river, righteousness like a never-
failing stream!*

—Amos 5:24

You know those icebreakers where you state an adjective that starts with the first letter of your name and describes you best? I used to pick "just," Just Jill. When I said that, I thought most people believed I used it to state that I am fair, unbiased, and honorable in my actions and leadership. I let them believe that, but actually, I used it to say I am just Jill, no one special, no need to consider me. I'm just Jill. How great is it to know when we say God is a Just God, we are not worshiping just a god! Instead, we are worshiping a Just God.

We love justice when bad people get what we think they deserve, but do we like justice when we are held accountable for our actions? Unfortunately, I don't think most of us can say that honestly. I'm so grateful, however, for a God who loves me enough to discipline me as a loving father would. My own experiences have taught me that justice in discipline is necessary for my development and my safety, and it draws me closer to God.

We are comfortable with a Just God when it is under the umbrella of justifiable discipline, but what about when our Just God's wrath is the catalyst for justice? The entire Old Testament speaks of a Just God whose wrath led to wars, plagues, and hardship for both the righteous and unrighteous. Even in our present day, we see God demonstrating His anger toward nations seeped in corruption. Here is what I believe.

Our Just God is also a jealous God. He has every reason to be jealous because He created us for Himself. But we have turned away from Him and chosen our ways over His ways. Consequently, our God experiences righteous anger. In our present time, while we live in a sinful world and are sinners, God's wrath is against sin, not people. He is sad when people sin, but He is not angry with them. He is executing His wrath against sin.

God loves everyone so much and does not want anyone to be eternally separated from Him. Thus, He passes judgment on sin to change our hearts and bring His people back to Him. Go back to the examples in the Old Testament, and see how His wrath led Israel to return to Him as their God every time.

It is true that people die in God's judgment on sin, but He gave plenty of warnings and opportunities to repent before He enacted His judgment.

The ends did justify His means since it always resulted in a revival among the people. Make no mistake, however; our Just God will judge people one day. The Book of Revelation tells us that every person who has ever been conceived will one day stand before God's judgment throne and give an account of their actions. As Christians whose sins are covered by the blood, we will not give an account of our sins, but rather we are accountable for what we did for God following our conversion. For the unsaved, however, will give an account of every sin they committed and will be reminded of each opportunity they had to accept Christ and His salvation yet chose not to do so. It is at this time that our Just God will enact justice and judgment, sending them to an eternal hell and separation from Him.

I am so grateful for my Just God. I'm thankful He holds me accountable out of love. I'm thankful He will one day judge us all and permanently eradicate sin. I wait with hope and excitement for a day when I will live in a new earth and a new heaven where sin does not exist. On that day, there will be no more pain, no more tears, and no more sorrow, for we will be made complete and whole.

Recommended worship:
"Move" by Jesus Culture

K – Knowing

Lord, you know everything there is to know about me. You perceive every movement of my heart and soul, and you understand my every thought before it even enters my mind. You are so intimately aware of me, Lord. You read my heart like an open book, and you know all the words I'm about to speak before I even start a sentence! You know every step I will take before my journey even begins.

—Ps. 139:1–4 TPT

He says, "Be still, and know that I am God; I will be exalted among the nations, I will be exalted in the earth."

—Ps. 46:10

We have heard it said, "Variety is the spice of life." That is so true especially as it relates to people. How boring would it be if we were all the same! Another cliché—"Opposites attract"—is also true. It's kind of funny how the things that irritate me the most in someone's life are traits I possess.

Although we are all uniquely different, each of us has a basic fundamental quality that God placed in us. It's the desire to be known by others—yes, even us introverts. We long to have someone know us and love us for who we are. God placed this desire in our hearts because He is a God of relationship, and He also wants to be known.

God knows everyone. He is a Knowing God. He knows you because He purposefully created you. He knows the number of hairs on your head (Matt. 10:30), He knows your name (Isa. 43:1), and He knows your every thought (Ps. 139:2). In fact, when you read the entire chapter of Psalm 139, you learn that He knows every detail about you—your thoughts and feelings, each genetic marker on your DNA, where you go to and fro, and your every hurt and joy. He knew you before you were conceived, and He knows what lies in your heart. He lovingly designed you as a beautiful masterpiece, and it's worth repeating—He knows you and loves you exactly as you are.

God's not satisfied with just knowing you. He wants to be known by you as well. There isn't much to a relationship if it is one-sided. To be known by someone is to know someone. The only way to truly know someone is to spend time with them. The more time you spend in their presence, talking and listening, the more you learn about them and the more they learn about you. A friendship develops. Invested time will lead to a strengthened relationship of love and intimacy. It's a beautiful thing.

Spending time with God begins with reading the Bible and praying, but there are many other ways to augment this quality time. For me, I grow in my knowledge of God through worship music and nature. It may and likely will be different for you.

I believe God displays Himself in the things you enjoy. After all, He designed you with those interests. If you're crafty, He will show up for you in those times you are creating something. If you enjoy music, you will discover Him there. The key, however, is to be still (in your heart, thoughts, and feelings). Take time during your favorite activity to quiet yourself. Be still and know your God.

I am grateful for a Knowing God who knows me personally. I feel loved; therefore, I want to know and love Him more.

Recommended worship:
"Know (Be Still)" by Jeremy Riddle;
"Known" by Tauren Wells

Day 12

L – Light

When Jesus spoke again to the people, he said, "I am the light of the world. Whoever follows me will never walk in darkness, but will have the light of life."

—John 8:12

He reveals deep and hidden things; he knows what lies in darkness, and light dwells with him.

—Dan. 2:22

The light shines in the darkness, and the darkness can never extinguish it.

—John 1:5 NLT

Can I let you in on a secret? I'm afraid of the dark. I hate not being able to see more than a few feet in front of me or around me. I don't consider myself a worrier, but there are many potential dangers of living in the dark. I'm so grateful for light. I especially love the sun. It is bright, warm, inviting, and comforting. It exposes the hidden things lurking in the dark. It defeats darkness even before it disappears over the horizon.

The sun that rises each day is great, but the real reward is the Son I get to wake up with every morning. Jesus, the Son of God, tells us in the above verse, "I am the light of the world." His presence in our life exposes the dark things hidden in our hearts and calls us to eliminate them. He's been doing that for me, exposing things like pride, jealousy, mistrust, and doubts. I've worked on removing these things, and His work in me brings me to worship as I remember his faithfulness. Still, there is one characteristic of the Light I will never forget.

From January through April of 2021, I was in a major spiritual battle of the mind. Satan began attacking my mind with negative thoughts, convincing me that I had no worth, that my walk with Christ was a fake, and that I would spend eternity separated from God. He used Matthew 7:21–23 to support those claims. For four months, the attacks were relentless, often accomplished by what felt like a legion of armies, until finally I submitted and gave Satan complete control of my mind. (Note: I am a child of God, and nothing can separate me from His love, so technically, Satan did not have complete control of my mind, but I no longer had any control.) The Sunday after I released my mind, I went to church against my will. Dave, my husband, essentially made me go. I remember being in complete darkness in my mind. It was scary and hopeless, and I was in unimaginable despair over my destiny. I broke down and sobbed.

Immediately, I saw a speck of light. It was like the tiniest star in a dark night sky, but that tiny light broke through the darkness so I could see it. I heard a voice say, "Focus on the light," so I did. The light grew bigger and bigger. I realized as it grew larger that my Savior was coming. That day, Jesus took my mind back from the enemy. My God of Light defeated darkness that day. He was faithful to His promise that He will never leave me or forsake me. Although I still fight battles in my mind, I know that He fights them for me. I know He is on the brink of complete dominion over darkness in my mind, and He gets all the glory and praise.

I am so grateful to my God of Light. He is bright, warm, and comforting. He defeats darkness and provides a lighted path where I can walk in obedience. I will always remember His faithfulness to me as the Light and will tell of His wonderful deeds.

Recommended worship:
"Let There Be Light" by Hillsong Worship

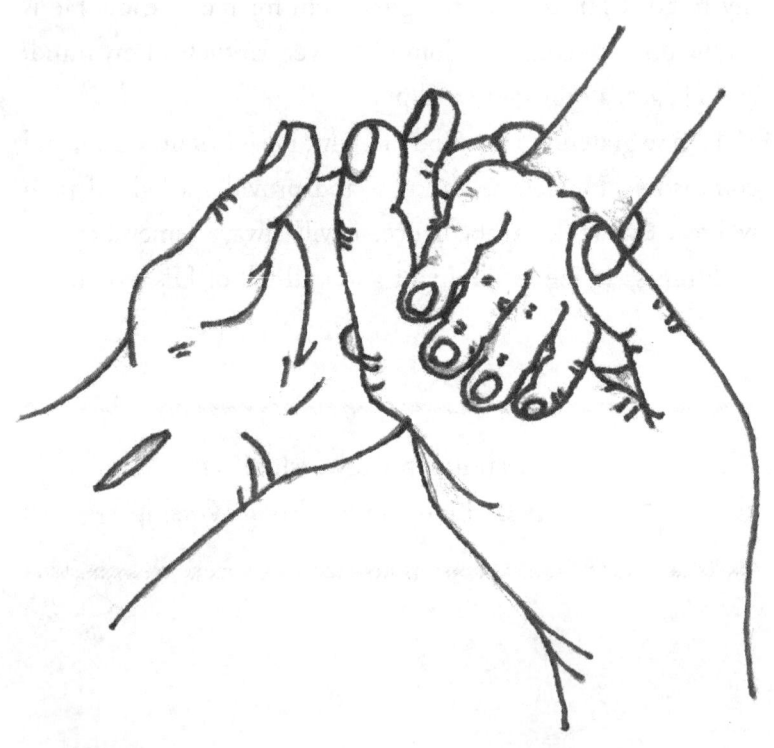

M – Mediator

For there is one God and one mediator between God and mankind, the man Christ Jesus.

—1 Tim. 2:5

For this reason, Christ is the mediator of a new covenant, that those who are called may receive the promised eternal inheritance—now that he has died as a ransom to set them free from the sins committed under the first covenant.

—Heb. 9:15

Jesus answered, "I am the way and the truth and the life. No one comes to the Father except through me."

—John 14:6

I don't like conflict and have been known to avoid it at times. I've learned from my leadership experience and my friendships that conflict avoidance only exacerbates problems and often causes more issues. The only real solution is conflict resolution, and when done respectfully and thoroughly, it will result in growth for all parties. However, sometimes the conflicting parties are unable to resolve their conflict on their own, thus making it necessary to bring in a mediator.

God created the world and everything in it and around it. All He made was perfect; there wasn't any conflict between God and mankind. When Adam and Eve sinned, it created a separation between God and mankind. Mankind's sin caused a conflict with God's holiness, and there was no resolving this conflict without a strategy. God gave mankind a temporary solution to reconcile Himself with them by establishing a covenant of blood sacrifices, but it was never capable of total resolution.

A covenant is an agreement or legal contract. Under the law of the old covenant, mankind's sin was always on them. The blood of their sacrifices was not capable of saving them, but they tried—until they didn't. Over time, their sacrifices were just a scapegoat that became mere religious rituals. Sadly, nearly 30 years of my Christian life were built on religious activities. I didn't intentionally receive God's grace. Unfortunately, I missed out on a relationship with Him.

Our loving God created us for relationship; therefore, He was not satisfied with a solution that was unable to resolve this conflict. Consequently, He needed to call in a mediator. There was only one who could fulfill that role—His Son, Jesus Christ. Jesus accepted the position, became a perfect man, and died as our blood offering. Christ's death and resurrection established a new covenant that enabled us to be reconciled to God. Those who receive Jesus as their Mediator are under the new covenant and are permanently reunited with God.

I am grateful for my God, the Mediator. Because of Jesus Christ, I am no longer in conflict with God. I am authorized to approach Him confidently at His throne. I will spend eternity with Him and He with me.

Recommended worship:
"One Mediator (Jesus the Only Way)"
by Cameron Keith

N – Near

Come near to God and he will come near to you. Wash your hands, you sinners, and purify your hearts, you double-minded.

—James 4:8

The Lord himself goes before you and will be with you; he will never leave you nor forsake you. Do not be afraid; do not be discouraged.

—Deut. 31:8

Over the course of the past 13 days, God has communicated a fairly prevalent theme to me. He loves you and wants to be in a relationship with you. Think about a relationship you value above others. What comes to mind? When I think about my close relationship, a few things come to mind—love, intimacy, time, and proximity, to name a few. To make a relationship function well, all these things are needed. Today, we will focus on proximity as we relate to a God who is Near.

God has given us several promises. First, if we draw near to Him, He will draw near to us. Second, He will never leave us or forsake us. I can attest to His faithfulness in both of these promises.

The first verse above tells us to draw near to God. We draw near to Him when we humble our hearts through prayer and worship. God always meets us when we spend quality time with Him. When we are in a position near Him, our perspectives are in line with His purpose, even when it doesn't make sense to us.

A few years ago, I was in a season when I was really walking in step with God. Every day I met with Him, and He met with me. I went out on a hike and came to a fork in the path. Long story short, I chose the wrong path and went with the seemingly most traveled. It was filled with many obstacles and struggles. God used this real-world situation to instruct me that the path everyone travels is not always the path He has for me or you to take. It doesn't make sense, but we are to trust. In November 2020, I reached another fork in the road. This time it was a decision about my future. I remembered the lesson from the hike and chose the path that didn't make sense. I had been close with God, so my perspective was aligned with His will. As I write this, I still do not understand all He did in this situation, but I know He is still near and working for my good.

It doesn't matter how long you may have been walking a Christian walk. There are times when we pull away from God or take our focus off of Him. We do it for one of two reasons. We are either scared and take our eyes off Christ to look at our circumstances, or we are too confident and turn our eyes inward. We serve a God, however, who never takes His eyes off of us. He is always near even when we do not feel His presence. I encourage you in those times to stop and consider this: "Where is my focus? Is it on the circumstances surrounding me, on myself, or on God?" If it's one of the first two, then turn your eyes back to Him through prayer and worship.

You will find Him there every time. If you are looking to Christ and He still feels distant, cling to His promise. He has not forsaken you. Trust Him as He works behind the scenes preparing you and others for what is to come next. He is faithful.

I am grateful for a God who is Near. I am confident of this because I have experienced times when He has drawn close to me and times when He has not forsaken me in my deepest time of need. If He is faithful to me, you can trust that He will be faithful to you.

Recommended worship:
"Your Nearness" by Shane & Shane;
"Draw Me Close" by Shane & Shane

O – Omni

You have searched me, Lord, and you know me. You know when I sit and when I rise; you perceive my thoughts from afar. You discern my going out and my lying down; you are familiar with all my ways. Before a word is on my tongue you, Lord, know it completely. You hem me in behind and before, and you lay your hand upon me. Such knowledge is too wonderful for me, too lofty for me to attain.

—Ps. 139:1–6

Where can I go from your Spirit? Where can I flee from your presence? If I go up to the heavens, you are there; if I make my bed in the depths, you are there. If I rise on the wings of the dawn, if I settle on the far side of the sea, even there your hand will guide me, your right hand will hold me fast. If I say, "Surely the darkness will hide me and the light become night around me," even the darkness will not be dark to you; the night will shine like the day, for darkness is as light to you.

—Ps. 139:7–12

For you created my inmost being; you knit me together in my mother's womb. I praise you because I am fearfully and wonderfully made; your works are wonderful, I know that full well. My frame was not hidden from you when I was made in the secret place, when I was woven together in the depths of the earth. Your eyes saw my unformed body; all the days ordained for me were written in your book before one of them came to be. How precious to me are your thoughts, God! How vast is the sum of them! Were I to count them, they would outnumber the grains of sand— when I awake, I am still with you.

—Ps. 139:13–18

Search me, God, and know my heart; test me and know my anxious thoughts. See if there is any offensive way in me, and lead me in the way everlasting.

—Ps. 139:23–24

God is one God in three persons—God the Father, Jesus the Son, and the Holy Spirit. This is a truth even seasoned Christians have a hard time understanding and explaining. We really don't need to nor should we try. I love that we serve a God we cannot comprehend. If I was able to know everything about Him, what would make Him so special? Discerning the Trinity is not the only thing about knowing God that is a challenge.

Understanding God's character is also challenging. He is so many things and has many character traits for which

I am grateful. We are already on the 15th attribute, but there are so many we will not be able to cover. Omniscient, omnipresent, and omnipotent are the hallmarks of God's quality traits. Unpacking these three traits in their totality is nearly impossible, but we can interpret enough to acknowledge how great our God is.

Omni is a prefix that means "all." Omniscient means God is all-knowing. Omnipresent means that God is in all places. Omnipotent means our God is all-powerful. One of my favorite chapters in the Bible is Psalm 139 because it reminds me how valued and beautiful I am to God. Until today, however, I did not realize how articulate David was in explaining these three characteristics of God.

Omniscient: God is ALL-KNOWING (Ps. 139:1—6)

I like to think I know quite a bit. Anyone who knows me and has studied the Enneagram personality test will recognize that I am a 5 on the Enneagram. What makes a 5 unique is a passion and an unquenchable thirst for knowledge. I have to know everything I can about a topic. If you and I are having a discussion and disagree or have differing thoughts, I will study the topic, usually to prove you wrong (because a 5 is always right) or to educate myself on the truth.

Despite how much knowledge I have, I do not know everything. But I serve a God who does. That's impressive. Of all the things God knows, what makes it personal is that He knows everything about me and you. The first six verses of

Psalm 139 humble me. He knows when I rise or sit. He knows my every thought even before I think it. He knows where I am going and when I sleep. And He knows what I am about to say even before it hits my tongue. His knowledge of me is too extensive for my brain to fathom. That is extremely hard for me to accept since I am a 5. It requires faith on my part, and it is what makes my God so special to me.

One thing I'd like to emphasize here is that God knows our every thought, feeling, and sin. We cannot hide them and keep them to ourselves. I know. I've tried. Even though I am a Christian, I never had complete freedom until I verbalized my every sin, thought, and feeling to God. There is power in exposing these things to His light by spoken word. Sadly, there are times I still attempt to hide it from Him, but freedom comes every time I voice whatever it is. Test me. Try it. Tell God verbally your every thought, feeling, and sin regardless of how bad you think they are, and let me know if you experience freedom. I'll be waiting to hear from you.

Omnipresent: God is ALL-PRESENT (Ps. 139:7–12)

God is everywhere. We cannot hide from Him. He lives in my heart, and if you profess Him as your Lord and Savior, He lives in your heart as well. He doesn't jump from me to you. He is everywhere. Verse 7 confirms that there is nowhere to hide from His Spirit. Neither heaven nor hell is inaccessible to Him. The distance from east to west is not too far from God. Whether I am in the darkness or the light, He is there keeping an eye on me. How comforting to know He is always by my side regardless of where I go or what circumstances I place myself in.

Omnipotent: God is ALL-POWERFUL (Ps. 139:13–18)

Our God is the creator of all things. Out of completely nothing, He made heaven and earth. He made light and darkness, forming the sun to guide the day and the moon for the evening. He separated the waters from above and below, establishing the sky and the seas. He separated the waters from the land and created all vegetation, creatures of the sea, land, and air. He created mankind in His own image. Science likes to define this as the Big Bang Theory. I don't disregard the fact that it was a big bang; we know from our Marvel and DC movies that power often is expressed as a flash or "big bang."

Our God is all-powerful and capable of doing anything. What He delights in is doing the impossible. It's when He demonstrates His power to us. I am currently in a position to see Him do the unimaginable. I've been struggling with something in my life that only God can change because it requires a heart transformation, and I am unable to renew it myself. It seems extra unlikely because many times I just don't want to change. I'm comfortable, I like it, and it only affects me (or so I tell myself), so change will require a renewal of not only my heart but my mind and feelings. Nevertheless, my desire above all else is to be holy as He is holy, so I'm expecting and anticipating Him to do the impossible. What is your impossible? Name it to God, and watch His power be displayed in you and for you.

I am grateful for a God who is All-Knowing, All-Present (everywhere), and All-Powerful. The last two verses say, "Lord, search me, test me, and send me." I have prayed this prayer several times in the past two years. It requires a lot of trust in an all-knowing, all-present, and all-powerful God to pray this prayer because He will answer it. It's been extremely difficult to walk it out, but oh, how great it is to see what He has done and continues to do. I am well on my way to becoming a new creation. Thank you, God, for being everything and ALL I need.

Recommended worship:
"Psalm 139 (Far Too Wonderful)" by Shane & Shane

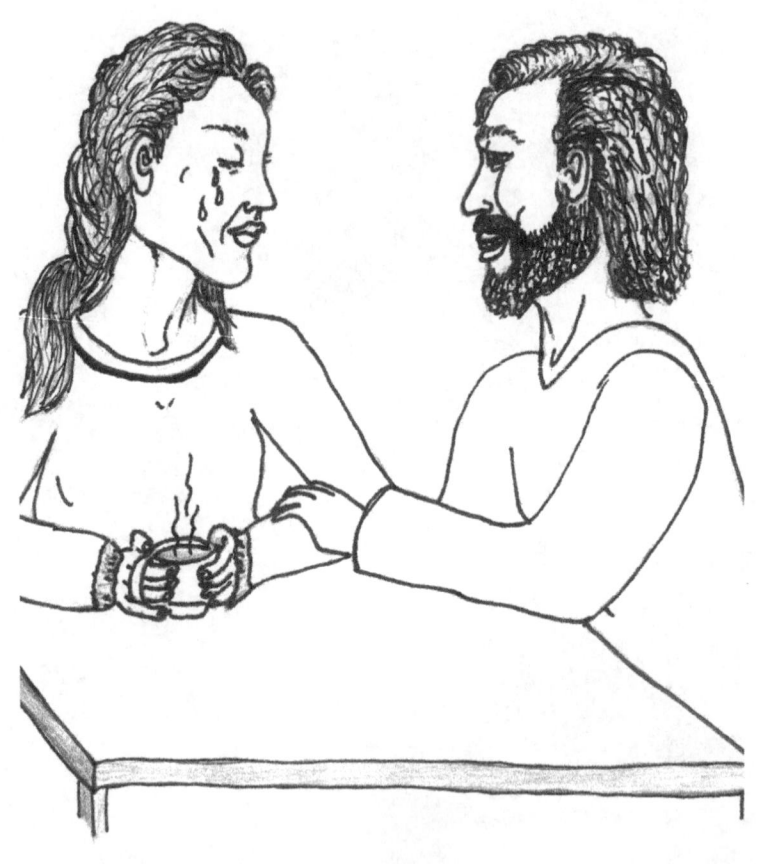

P – Pursuer

Then the man and his wife heard the sound of the Lord God as he was walking in the garden in the cool of the day, and they hid from the Lord God among the trees of the garden. But the Lord God called to the man, "Where are you?"

—Gen. 3:8–9

Surely your goodness and unfailing love will pursue me all the days of my life, and I will live in the house of the Lord forever.

—Ps. 23:6 NLT

Parables of God pursuing lost sheep (Luke 15:1–7), a lost coin (Luke 15:8–10), and a lost son (Luke 15:11–32)

Have you ever lost something precious to you and tore your house apart looking for it? Think about how passionate or committed you were to finding it. How did it make you feel when you found it or didn't find it? Imagine that same passion and commitment of someone pursuing you with a love so deep they will go to any lengths to find you, heal you, and bring you into his family. Our God, the Pursuer, is He.

The entire Bible is littered with stories of God pursuing us when we run away from Him. It starts in the third chapter of Genesis. Adam and Eve walked with God daily, but one day they sinned. In their shame, they ran and hid from God. His response was this: "Where are you?" We know from yesterday that God is all-knowing, so why did He ask Adam where he was? Brokenhearted, God was really asking, "Why are you spiritually out of alignment in our relationship, and why did you run and hide from me instead of seeking me?" God knew Adam and Eve sinned. He could have left them and us in sin, but He didn't because He loves us so much. He will search for us to the ends of the earth and bring us into right relationship with Him.

What is great about the God who pursues is His relentlessness. As a result of His love for us, God never grows tired. He will pursue and woo you until your last breath. If you have never accepted Christ as your Savior, He is running after you right now. You probably have not realized it is Him, but He is present in what you would consider your conscience. He speaks to you in your thoughts or feelings, beckoning you to be in relationship with Him. Simply acknowledge Jesus as God, confess that you are a sinner, repent (tell Him you're sorry), and admit that He is the only one who can save you from eternal death. Then tell someone—a Christian family member, a friend, or a pastor. Let them celebrate in your new freedom and advise you on the next steps as you start the best relationship you will ever be in. God and all those in heaven will rejoice in your salvation. How cool is it to know that a celebration is happening in heaven the moment you turn your life over to Christ!

For those of us who are saved, God pursues us for relationship, especially when we sin. He does not want our relationship to be severed. Just like with Adam, He asks us, "Where are you?" as His Holy Spirit convicts us. Simply turn back to Him, and receive His grace. Just like with new Christians, heaven rejoices at our acceptance of God's grace.

I am grateful for a God who Pursues me. Too often I need Him to come after me as I hide from my sinful ways and feel shame. Faithfully, He continues to pursue me until I am found and set back into spiritual alignment with Him.

Recommended worship:
"The 99" by 7eventh Time Down; "You Keep Coming after Me" by Austin Stone Worship

Q – Quantity

"I am the Alpha and the Omega," says the Lord God, "who is, and who was, and who is to come, the Almighty."

—Rev. 1:8

There is a season (a time appointed) for everything and a time for every delight and *event* or *purpose under heaven.*

—Eccles. 3:1 AMP

In the beginning the Word [Jesus] already existed. The Word was with God, and the Word was God. *He existed in the beginning with God. God created everything through him, and nothing was created except through him. The Word gave life to everything that was created, and his life brought light to everyone.* (emphasis added)

—John 1:1–4 NLT

erriam Webster defines quantity in these three ways: 1. an indefinite amount or number; 2. a determinate or estimated amount; and 3. a total amount or number. We are about to discover that God is a God of Quantity. He is infinite, has a set time for everything, and is complete (total). He is everything we need, and the only one we need.

1. *an indefinite amount or number.* For all the mathematical physics lovers out there, let's not get into a debate between the subtle nuances between indefinite and infinite. For this discussion, they are synonymous. God is infinite and indefinite. In other words, He has always been in existence, and He always will be. There are no boundaries to His existence. Our human mind can comprehend to a small degree that His future existence is infinite, but no way can we wrap our brains around the fact that He has always been here. We serve a God who cannot be explained. The world sees that as a problem, but I celebrate the fact that my God is mysterious. That makes Him even more significant because I cannot put Him in a box like other gods. What's so special about a fertility god or sun god? They are one-dimensional. I serve a God who is everything at all times, exactly when I need Him.

2. *a determinate or estimated amount.* God is not defined by time, but we are. Second Peter 3:8 tells us that a day is as a thousand years to the Lord, and a thousand years are but one day to Him. Regardless of the timeline, King Solomon tells us that God has a time for everything. Can I let you in on a secret? This part of His character frustrates me to

no end. I am not a very patient person when I want something. At times I manipulate and connive to get what I want. That does not work in God's system of timing. His timing is perfect and right on time every time. Looking at 2 Peter 3:9, we see that "the Lord is not slow in keeping His promise, as some understand slowness. Instead, he is patient with you, not wanting anyone to perish, but everyone to come to repentance." Wow! He is a God who loves us so much that He is willing to wait on eternity so He can give everyone an opportunity to join Him.

3. *total amount or number.* God loves numbers, and He loves patterns. In God's numerology system, completeness or perfection is seen in the numbers 1, 3, and 7. "The number 1 is only divisible by itself. It is independent of any other numerals yet composes them all" (biblestudy.org). We serve one God. He is complete in every way. The number 3 is seen hundreds of times in Scripture, but the most important use of the number is in reference to the Trinity, one God in three persons—God the Father, Jesus the Son, and the Holy Spirit. This is another mysterious attribute we cannot fully grasp. We believe it to be true because God has been faithful in all His previous words; therefore, we can trust what He says. The numbers 3 and 7 are the most written numbers in the book of Revelation.

"Seven is the number of completeness and perfection (both physical and spiritual). It derives much of its meaning from being tied directly to God's creation of all things" (biblestudy. org). Here are some additional facts:

The Bible, as a whole, was originally divided into 7 major divisions. They are 1) the Law; 2) the Prophets; 3) the Writings, or Psalms; 4) the Gospels and Acts; 5) the General Epistles; 6) the Epistles of Paul; and 7) the book of Revelation. The total number of originally inspired books was forty-nine, or 7 x 7, demonstrating the absolute perfection of the Word of God. In the book of Revelation there are seven churches, seven angels to the seven churches, seven seals, seven trumpet plagues, seven thunders, and the seven last plagues. The first resurrection of the dead takes place at the 7th trumpet, completing salvation for the Church.*

I am so grateful that God is a God of Quantity. I do not think you will find quantity in any other character trait discussion, but I felt led to show you this aspect of God. In short, He is incomprehensible, mysterious, unexplainable, and yet everything you need, infinitely full of love, compassion,

---

* "Meaning of Numbers in the Bible: The Number 7," biblestudy. org," Accessed November 16, 2021, at https://www.biblestudy.org/bibleref/meaning-of-numbers-in-bible/7.html.

mercy, and grace. He is complete in who He is and perfect in His timing.

Recommended worship:
"Christ Is Enough" by Hillsong Worship

R – Rest

Come to me, all you who are weary and burdened, and I will give you rest. Take my yoke upon you and learn from me, for I am gentle and humble in heart, and you will find rest for your souls.

—Matt. 11:28–29

On the seventh day God had finished his work of creation, so he rested from all his work. And God blessed the seventh day and declared it holy, because it was the day when he rested from all his work of creation.

—Gen. 2:2–3 NLT

My two favorite pastimes are eating and sleeping. I can do those two activities all day long and be content. Earlier I mentioned that I am a 5 on the Enneagram personality test. Not only do I like to research, but I love and protect my alone time—all the time. In my alone time, I dedicate an hour for rest. Sometimes I sleep, but mostly I spend it in worship with God.

God wants rest for us. He knows how important it is to all phases of our human makeup—spiritual, physical, mental, and even social health. When God calls us to rest, He is telling us to lay down what we are doing and the burdens we are carrying. There is only one place we will find true rest—with Jesus at the cross.

I grew up in a Christian home, and Sundays were our day of rest. On that day, we didn't work and minimized our play activities and things such as shopping. We spent the time fellowshipping with friends or family and taking naps between morning and evening church services. We did that because God rested and instructed us to do so too. God did not rest because He had to; He never grows tired. He rested because He was setting an example for us, knowing that without rest we would grow weary. As a child, I hated Sundays. I did not understand or value the importance of rest.

Today, I seek it daily, not just on Sundays.

Sunday is not just about finding a day to stop working and doing activities. It's about seeking God, giving all our worries, stresses, and burdens to Him, slowing down our lives enough to see and spend time with Christ, and recharging our spirits and our physical, mental, and social components. It's nearly impossible to do any of those things when we are constantly on the go and allocating all our time to others or to things.

In the first verses above, Jesus said to take His yoke, and you'll find rest for your soul. For those unfamiliar with a yoke, it is a harness with two loops placed on oxen to pull the weight of something. One loop is bigger than the other because a strong ox and a weak ox are paired together. The strong ox bears most of the burden. Jesus is our strong ox and shoulders the weight of our struggles when we pair up with Him.

Something struck me for the first time as I wrote this. When Jesus was going to the cross to be crucified, He carried the horizontal piece of the cross on His shoulders. He was crucified for our sins, and the cross is the literal and symbolic demonstration of that. Consequently, by carrying the burden of the cross on His shoulder, He chose to singlehandedly, with a single yoke, carry our sins, burdens, worries, and fears on His shoulders. I'm not discounting what Jesus said about the yoke, but what I recognize is that if I go to the cross, I can give it all to Christ. He's already carried it for me; I don't need to take it back. David knew this as well when he said, "Truly my soul finds rest in God; my salvation comes from Him" (Ps. 62:1).

I am grateful for a God who Rested. He loves us so much that He did something He did not need to do so we will follow His example and be free from our burdens. Jesus is our resting place. Seek Him daily, and you will find true rest. You will be healthier spiritually and mentally. Your relationships will be healthier, and you will be less prone to physical fatigue.

Recommended worship:
"Only There" by Shane & Shane;
"The Gospel Is Rest" by Elias Dummer

S - Shepherd

All of us, like sheep, have strayed away. We have left God's paths to follow our own. Yet the Lord laid on him the sins of us all.

—Isa. 53:6 NLT

The Lord is my shepherd, I lack nothing. He makes me lie down in green pastures, he leads me beside quiet waters, he refreshes my soul. He guides me along the right paths for his name's sake. Even though I walk through the darkest valley, I will fear no evil, for you are with me; your rod and your staff, they comfort me. You prepare a table before me in the presence of my enemies. You anoint my head with oil; my cup overflows. Surely your goodness and love will follow me all the days of my life, and I will dwell in the house of the Lord forever.

—Ps. 23:1– 6

I am the good shepherd. The good shepherd lays down his life for the sheep. I am the good shepherd; I know my sheep and my sheep know me.

—John 10:11, 14

I'm going to go out on a limb and say that most of us do not know very many shepherds. It's also probably a safe bet that many of us do not even know what a shepherd does other than hang out with sheep all day. Being a shepherd was considered a lowly job delegated typically to the youngest boy in a family. I find that interesting because sheep were extremely important to the spiritual and physical welfare of the Jewish people. Spiritually speaking, lambs were used in offering sacrifices in order to cleanse the people of sin, give thanks to God, and fellowship among friends and family. Physical reliance came in the form of meat, milk, and wool for clothing. The sheep provided these necessities for the family, but sheep were also their primary source of income.

A shepherd was responsible for caring for the family's sheep. Caring for them involved feeding them, leading them to rest, ensuring they had clean water, sheltering them, protecting the sheep from predators, pouring oil on their heads, and maintaining the health of each sheep or lamb.

Additionally, they assisted the ewes in birthing lambs. The shepherd's path to success not only depended on tending the flock but also on caring and having compassion for the individual sheep. There were usually over a thousand sheep, and the shepherd knew each sheep and lamb individually. The shepherd was thus more capable of identifying, which ones were sick, injured, orphaned, happy, or sad.

Sheep are often considered the dumbest animals because they are prone to wander, have poor eyesight, and tend to get themselves into trouble a lot. But can an animal really be all that dumb if it is able to survive thousands of years? Sheep are the oldest living domesticated animal on earth, dating back over 5,000 years. Additionally, sheep know how to recognize their shepherd's voice and will only listen to him.

Sheep do tend to make themselves look dumb—hence the moniker. They wander off frequently since they are always seeking something better—like greener grass. I suppose that's where this phrase came from: "The grass is always greener on the other side of the fence." I'm sure that was in one of David's psalms—probably verse 7 of Psalm 23! Wandering off to find greener pastures placed the sheep in harmful situations where they were easy prey for predators. That often led to injury or death.

We are just like sheep. In fact, the Lord says we are all sheep who have gone astray. We seek after things such as sex, alcohol, drugs, the need to perform, seeking achievement and accolades, pornography, chasing perfection, always being in control, avoiding conflict, and more. These only give us temporary happiness but always lead us right into the jaws of our predator, Satan. Our fleshly pleasures ultimately cause deep wounds and death. When the Good Shepherd comes to find and rescue us from the devil and we follow Him is when we will find true happiness.

One of the most well-known chapters of the Bible is Psalm 23. In it, David, a shepherd boy himself, recognized God as our Shepherd. Jesus confirmed this when He said, "I am the Good Shepherd" (John 10:11). Looking at Psalm 23, we see all the evidence of God as our Good Shepherd. He gives His sheep (us) everything they need; we lack nothing. He leads us to plush pastures so we can rest. He leads us to still waters (Jesus is our living water). He guides us on the right path so we are not in predator territory, and we have just the right resources for today. He comforts us with His rod (used to defend from predators) and staff (used to redirect), and He anoints our heads with oil (prevents sunstroke and parasites from entering eyes, ears, and nose).

I am grateful for Jehovah Ra'ah, God my Shepherd (fun fact: Ra'ah is a derivative of Rea', which means "friend"). All too often I find myself wandering toward those things I believe will bring me happiness only to find myself in the clutches of shame and condemnation. My Shepherd and Friend is faithful to come after me every time and bring me back into the fold.

Recommended worship:
"Shepherd" by Highlands Worship

T – Transform

Create in me a pure heart, O God, and renew a steadfast spirit within me.

—Ps. 51:10

Throw off your old sinful nature and your former way of life, which is corrupted by lust and deception. Instead, let the Spirit renew your thoughts and attitudes. Put on your new nature, created to be like God—truly righteous and holy.

—Eph. 4:22–24 NLT

And we all, who with unveiled faces contemplate the Lord's glory, are being transformed into his image with ever-increasing glory, which comes from the Lord, who is the Spirit.

—2 Cor. 3:18

It's time to get real with y'all because I have a story to tell. This is God's story of transformation, so give Him the glory. For 50 years I did not believe Jesus's death and resurrection were a sacrifice at all. First, He was God. While His human form felt pain, He knew He would rise again and defeat death; therefore, I just never thought it was a big deal. Additionally, I didn't really believe I was a sinner. I was told growing up in church that I was a sinner, but I was a good girl, so Christ's death didn't mean anything to me personally since I hadn't done anything all that bad.

After I recommitted my life to Christ in 2014, there didn't seem to be a lot of growth in my spiritual walk. I came to realize it was due to these two beliefs. I decided to start praying that God would let me see myself as a sinner through His eyes. Simultaneously, I read a book called *Dangerous Prayers* and started praying that God would search my heart for sin, break me to the point I would put away those sins, and send me out to tell people what He did. What I learned six months later was to be careful about what you pray because God will answer you! Much of this you have gotten in the past 19 days, but it is all together here. Now let's look at God's transforming work in my life.

This transforming journey actually started six years prior to what I believed was the starting point. I prayed for years that God would send me a spiritual friend. Instead, He prepared me to receive a friend who would be my vulnerability partner and so much more. Before I could be vulnerable with an earthly friend, I needed to become vulnerable with my heavenly friend, Jesus. In August 2020, I finally surrendered and told Jesus all my hurts, my frustrations, and my anger toward Him for allowing things to happen in my life. I just word-vomited every thought and feeling I had carried for 50 years. That was what He had been waiting for and was ready with open arms.

Within days, God revealed how broken I was from my past. Honestly, I didn't think I was broken. Things like childhood sexual abuse and parental emotional detachment occurred in my childhood, but I had dealt with it as an adult and moved on. In hindsight, I knew that was false because I had built so many walls up around my heart. It affected everyone I came in contact with. I did not get emotionally attached to anyone, even my family, and definitely not anyone outside my family. I was broken, seemingly healed by my own accord but still in a lot of pain and dysfunction. God was about to take this brokenness, heal me, and transform me into something completely foreign to me—someone who loves and is compassionate, humble, and pure in thoughts and deeds. Nevertheless, I could not do that without someone to walk alongside me.

I started attending Megan's small group, a weekly Bible study. During that year, God slowly worked on softening my heart toward Megan, thus building a level of trust I would need to share my darkest pains and sins. God chose Megan to walk with me, so I (rather God through me) gave her the Hebrew name Bachir, which means "chosen one."

In the final days of August 2020, I shared things with Megan that I had never shared with anyone else. I shared my hurts. What seemed very scary that day turned out to be extremely freeing. I thought that was it and that I was healed. Oh, naïve me! It was less than a week when God opened my eyes to how my past hurts had led me to dishonor Him by my sinful actions. That was the first installment of seeing my sin through His eyes. All the little sins I thought were of no significance were displayed in front of me as Christ hung on the cross completely separated from His Father. No one can really fathom what this truly means, but that day, I felt it. I immediately recognized what Christ sacrificed for each of these sins. "My God, my God, why have you forsaken me?" (Ps. 22:1), He cried out as the union between Him and His Father became severed, and it was all because of my sins. Bachir was there to comfort and encourage me and point me back to the fact that Christ did it because He loved me that much. Who loves like that? Christ does!

The following day, Megan, her sister, and I went on a hike to a spring. I asked my husband to make me a small, wooden cross about 1'6" in size. At the spring, I had all my sins written on small Post-it notes and nailed them to the cross. It was a symbolic activity for me that gave me permission to release the shame of the sins God had revealed, and it worked. For weeks I felt free and was ready to go tell everyone what God had done. Search me, break me, and now send me. "Oh, child," God said, "we have more work to do."

Between September and December, God exhorted my heart to surrender. Sadly, the very gift He gave me became my idol. I never allowed myself to get emotionally attached to anyone, so I had never had a real friendship. Being vulnerable with Megan led me into an emotional attachment I was too inexperienced to know how to prioritize. Consequently, instead of recognizing what God was doing through her, I gave her all the credit and placed her on God's throne. It took a lot of tears and trials to release her and remove her from the throne, but

I'm grateful for a patient God who created a way for us to remain friends.

As the calendar turned to 2021, I began having major spiritual attacks on my mind. Despite having studied spiritual warfare for two years prior, I did not defend it well. As a result, the attacks got worse and more intense until I finally gave up control and handed it over to Satan. It was never mine to give away, however, so Jesus took back what was His. I still struggle even now with negative thoughts that send me into spirals at times, but they are becoming less and less frequent. I have learned to identify the lies Satan throws at me and defend them with God's truth.

The next several months were fairly quiet as I prepared for retirement, although God began laying the foundation of what work we were about to venture into—my value and significance, mistrust, faith, and the big work of pride and lust. He knew I would need time to walk through these things and find freedom.

July began with a struggle about my worth and significance. I felt like I didn't have any value to bring to people, and hence I didn't trust them. As God explored this thought with me, He showed me it was really rooted in a mistrust of Him. How can I trust a God who allowed a child of three years old to be sexually assaulted, not just once but multiple times by multiple perpetrators spanning ten years?

Here I am again, healing from my past. I thought God and I worked through this last year. As with any wound, it takes time. Most of the work is being done under the scab, but the scab stays around for a long time before new skin replaces it. That is where I am in my healing.

Toward the end of July, I was struggling with the things God had been working on and decided to go on a three-day spiritual retreat in the woods. I removed all distractions of electronics and people so I could spend time with God. I went into the retreat with an agenda and came out with God's. There were two major themes I took away from that retreat. The independence I so proudly flaunted had me bound and chained. My independence prevented me from relying on God and His strength in the working of my sins and healing. Along with independence, He introduced pride and the need to humble myself.

Upon returning home, God, Bachir, and I began working on mistrust, followed quickly by faith. I prayed many times for more faith, yet I was never given more. Through this walk, God informed me that I had all the faith I needed, but I was not activating it. I did not trust God to come through on faith in my life. Essentially, I was calling Him a liar. We worked on those two things for a few weeks until I reached a level of trust and faith to move on. All this extra time when I didn't have a job afforded God an opportunity to reveal the two sins in my heart that had taken root and unknowingly controlled me. Those sins were pride and lust. A couple of months before at the spiritual retreat, He identified pride to me, but He was about to reveal how it ruled my life.

My husband and I bought a house. The house has a patio in front with a lot of greenery. I didn't want all that greenery because I wanted to place a rock garden with remembrance rocks in it. As I dug up the greenery, I came upon some roots from a tree on the other side of the fence. The roots were deep and thick, and traveled under the patio. God used those roots to reveal the extent of pride in my heart. I learned that pride is the source of many other root sins I possess such as jealousy, control, mistrust, unforgiveness, lust, and doubt, to name a few.

He also opened my eyes to how pride was the motive driving many of my behaviors, even the ones I thought honored Him. I quickly asked Him to remove pride from me. His response? It will require me to step out in obedience. The obedience He commanded came in the form of humility as I was to seek forgiveness from multiple people on whom my pride had had the largest negative impact.

As I continued to work on pride and sought forgiveness, God convicted me of lust. In the process of transforming me, He gave me tools and building blocks to help prepare for the next areas of work—trust, surrender, and obedience. At each step along the way, God used Bachir to walk with me on this journey. It is not easy to be so open about my sins, but I learned there is victory in vulnerability and freedom in friendship, especially when joined together by God.

Prior to this, I believed I was in a place of spiritual, emotional, and mental health. The years on this healing path have revealed lies that blind me. I am grateful for a God who Transforms. His process is almost always difficult but also rewarding to release and break down each of these strongholds. His ways are slow and methodical, allowing me to take small steps of obedience as He slowly changed me from the inside out.

Shortly after I gave Megan the name Bachir, she gave me the Hebrew name Chadash, which means "renewed." I love that name; I am a new creation.

Recommended worship:
"Just One Touch" by Kim Walker-Smith;
"Just One Touch" by Planetshakers

U – Unchanging

I the Lord do not change.

—Mal. 3:6

Jesus Christ is the same yesterday and today and forever.

—Heb. 13:8

The grass withers and the flowers fall, but the word of our God endures forever.

—Isa. 40:8

Raise your hand if you like change. My hand is partly raised. There are some things I think need changing and some things I am quite content leaving as is. I do not like change when it's done just for the sake of change. However, I've learned from my time in leadership that there are often situations when change is good and necessary for individual and organizational growth. It prevents stagnation and sparks innovation. Yet change is not good when leaders modify their positions as circumstances fluctuate. That causes chaos, and people will not know the standard by which to live and work.

One thing we can be certain of is that God does not change Himself or His position—ever. He is the same yesterday and today, and we can be 100 percent confident He will remain the same tomorrow. He gave us His standards and instructions in the Bible, and He will never change His mind to reflect our New Age philosophies. Sadly, we want to change His Word using the argument that God loves us all regardless of what we do and how we choose to live our lives. That statement that He loves us is completely 100 percent accurate; however, He does not change His standard of what sin is in order to show love. In fact, it is by maintaining His truth of what is sin and what is holy that He affirms how much He loves us.

God does not change, but change is good and necessary for us. We were made in the image of Christ. For a long time, I thought that meant a human body, but God is not human. Christ came to earth and took a human body, but prior to that, He was and is spirit. When the Bible says we are made in the image of God, it means we are created in spirit by the Spirit and given His attributes. We've studied God's character these past 21 days, and except for the Omni characteristics, we also have all these characteristics. Unfortunately, our sin distorted, damaged, and repressed them. When we become saved, God begins restoring us to His original design for us, and we begin to look more and more like Christ. I love my renewed self and the restoration of traits I failed to recognize before. I love people and myself better, I have more compassion for others, my mind (which I'm learning is a gift) is full of positive thoughts and not critical lies about myself and others, and I have more joy, peace, gentleness, and kindness in my heart.

I am grateful to serve a God who is Unchanging. I am grateful that my Unchanging God recognizes my need to change and guides me in it.

Recommended worship:
"Unchanging" by Chris Tomlin

Day 22

V – Vinedresser/Vine

Abide in me, and I in you. As the branch cannot bear fruit by itself, unless it abides in the vine, neither can you, unless you abide in me. I am the vine; you are the branches. Whoever abides in me and I in him, he it is that bears much fruit, for apart from me you can do nothing.

—John 15:4– 5 ESV

No one has ever seen God; if we love one another, God abides in us, and his love is perfected in us. By this we know that we abide in him and he in us, because he has given us of his Spirit. Whoever confesses that Jesus is the Son of God, God abides in him, and he in God. So we have come to know and to believe the love that God has for us. God is love, and whoever abides in love abides in God, and God abides in him. By this is love perfected with us, . . . There is no fear in love, but perfect love casts out fear. For fear has to do with punishment, and whoever fears has not been perfected in love. We love because he first loved us.

—1 John 4:12–13, 15–19 ESV

But the Holy Spirit produces this kind of fruit in our lives: love, joy, peace, patience, kindness, goodness, faithfulness, gentleness, and self-control. There is no law against these things!

—Gal. 5:22–23 NLT

Growing up in Ohio afforded me access to a lot of fruit in the wild. I often went out with buckets and harvested raspberries, elderberries, grapes, and more. Grapes were the easiest to harvest because they came in clusters. Grapevines were easy to identify; however, it wasn't until I lived in California that I really noticed grapevines and their construction.

As Jesus and His disciples walked to the garden for the last time, Jesus talked about a vineyard along the way. He told them that His Father is the vinedresser, He is the vine, and we are the branches. I didn't quite understand the makeup of a grapevine in this manner because the grapevines in the wild are not groomed; therefore, their tendrils are all over the place. In a vineyard where the plants are groomed, the grapevines are maintained so the tendrils are high above the ground, about three feet. Being off the ground produces the maximum amount of fruit because they have more access to sunlight, air circulates around them, they are not bogged down by dirt and grime, and they do not get trampled on. When viewing a maintained vine, it appears much like a small tree.

Jesus said that He is the vine. Previously, I thought the vine was the tendrils, but it isn't. The vine is the main source of nutrients and thus life. It looks a lot like a tree trunk. Jesus said we are the branches—the tendrils that bear the fruit. If a branch breaks and falls off, it will die, and no fruit will form. If a branch breaks but doesn't fall off, the vinedresser can quickly secure it to the vine again, allowing it to reattach and bear fruit. If the branch falls to the ground, the vinedresser lovingly picks it up, cleans it off, and secures it to the other branches where it can again bear fruit.

Jesus's final teaching before his death emphasized the importance of our abiding in Him. Jesus is our source of life. How do we abide in Him? We rest in His Word, the Bible. We pray to Him. We worship Him with songs. We think about Him throughout the day. We go to Him for advice, decision-making, small talk, and deep conversation. We depend on Him for everything—our strength, our love, our courage, and our daily provisions of food, shelter, and clothing. Everything we need, He supplies. We just have to depend on Him and thank Him when He does provide, even when it doesn't look like our expectations.

God is our vinedresser. He keeps an eye on us and lovingly prunes us, cleans us off when we fall, and fixes our broken pieces. He attaches us to other branches who give us support, protects us from the wind, face storms together, and ensure that we stay attached, abiding in the vine. God loves us perfectly; therefore, we have nothing to fear as we grow and produce fruit in service to Him. Additionally, He gives us a helper, the Holy Spirit, when we remain in Him. The Holy Spirit is the one who gives and ripens our fruit. You can always tell when a person is healthy and abiding in Jesus by their fruit. These fruits are easily recognizable. They are love, joy, peace, patience, kindness, goodness, faithfulness, gentleness, and self-control.

I am grateful for Jesus, my vine who I depend on, and for God my vinedresser who watches over me and keeps me attached to the vine. As I intentionally seek to abide in Jesus, I recognize how abundant my fruit is. I always want my life to have a plentiful harvest and a basket that overflows with fruit.

Recommended worship:
"Abide in Me" by Andrew Marcus;
"Abide" by Aaron Williams

W – Walk

Then the man and his wife heard the sound of the Lord God as he was walking in the garden in the cool of the day, and they hid from the Lord God among the trees of the garden.

—Gen. 3:8

I will walk among you and be your God, and you will be my people.

—Lev. 26:12

And your ears shall hear a word behind you, saying, "This is the way, walk in it," when you turn to the right or when you turn to the left.

—Isa. 30:21 ESV

I enjoy going on walks and hikes. I will go regardless of the season; I just have to dress appropriately for the weather. Normally these activities are much more enjoyable when I have someone to talk with. Time and temperature no longer become relevant when there is someone beside me. They help keep my mind off the cold, heat, rain, or snow.

I'm not the only one who likes to get out and walk. God

also likes to take walks, and He enjoys having a partner with Him as well. From the beginning of time as we know it, God desired to walk with us. He spent many days in the Garden of Eden with Adam and Eve. Genesis 3:8 gives us a glimpse into His heart. In case we cannot see His longing to walk and be with us, He tells us, "I will walk among you and be your God, and you will be my people" (Lev. 26:12).

God loves to walk with us because He enjoys our company; however, there is another reason. He is not a silent walking partner. He wants to talk with us on our journey. I said I enjoy walking with people, but often I am by myself. During those seemingly solo walks, I am never alone. God and I are out together. We have some of the best conversations on these walks. I seek His direction, praise Him, vent, and laugh with Him. We engage in small talk, but most of the time we have some very deep conversations. I ask Him questions about my struggles and who He is, and He always answers me. When I'm not seeking answers to my questions, He speaks softly and encourages me, guides me, expresses His love for me, and is just a wonderful walking partner.

I am grateful for a God who Walks with me, a God who desires to spend time with me and calls me to walk with Him. I think I'm going to go for a walk.

Recommended worship:
"Walk with You" by SEU Worship

Day 24

X – eXhortation

All Scripture is inspired by God and is useful to teach us what is true and to make us realize what is wrong in our lives. It corrects us when we are wrong and teaches us to do what is right. God uses it to prepare and equip his people to do every good work.

—2 Tim. 3:16–17 NLT

Preach the word; be ready in season and out of season; reprove, rebuke, and exhort, with complete patience and teaching.

—2 Tim. 4:2 ESV

[E]encourage the hearts of your fellow believers and support one another, just as you have already been doing. We appeal to you, dear brothers and sisters, to instruct those who are not in their place of battle. Be skilled at gently encouraging those who feel themselves inadequate. Be faithful to stand your ground. Help the weak to stand again. Be quick to demonstrate patience with everyone.

—1 Thess. 5:11, 14 TPT

*P*araklesis is the Greek word for "exhortation." *Para* means "to be close." *Klesis* is "to call." A good, biblical definition of *exhortation* is "admonishing and encouraging someone up close and personal." God is a God who exhorts us, but we have to be close to Him in order to hear His voice. Reading the Bible is the primary avenue God uses to exhort us. When we look at the above verse in 2 Timothy, we see that He uses His Word to admonish and encourage us up close and personal. Yesterday, we talked about God walking and talking with us. He exhorts us all the time when we quiet ourselves and listen. It's not an audible voice, but He speaks to us in our thoughts and feelings. If you tend to think more than feel, He will talk as your thoughts. If you are someone who feels more than you think, He will communicate to you through your feelings.

Since we are to be like God, He desires us to exhort others. Anyone can exhort another and is encouraged to do so as seen in the above verses and many others in the Bible. Nevertheless, exhortation is also one of the gifts of the Holy Spirit. I have the gift of exhortation. The difference between the gift and regular exhortation is that the one with a gift recognizes the need to exhort in a deeper, more specific way.

The primary, motivational drive of the gift is to encourage believers to mature in Christ. Just like location, location, location is important when buying a house, encourage, encourage, encourage is important to an exhorter. However, exhortation is not just encouraging; it's also admonishing and correcting your beliefs and behavior. Exhortation is great when we can encourage, but it's challenging to correct someone, especially if they are not receptive to it. It's also extremely important to follow the Holy Spirit's prompting and not go it alone. I've learned the hard way that exhorting at the wrong time can lead to broken relationships and hinder someone's growth.

There are multiple ways you can exhort someone. Most common is through speaking to the person. I love worship music, so that is my customary way to encourage people. I send someone songs that speak to the season they are in at the time. Other ways are by your service (cooking meals, being available, visiting at the hospital, etc.).

I'm grateful for a God who eXhorts. He has taught me the correct way and gifted me to draw others to Him. I go into eXhortation with the premise that I will bless a person but always come out being blessed in return. If the opportunity presents itself, I'm hopeful that you, too, will encourage someone close to you.

Recommended worship:
"Speak" by Bethany Music;
"Speak to Me" by Kathryn Scott

Day 25

Y – Yield

He was saying to them, "The harvest is abundant [for there are many who need to hear the good news about salvation], but the workers [those available to proclaim the message of salvation] are few. Therefore, [prayerfully] ask the Lord of the harvest to send out workers into His harvest. Go your way; listen carefully: I am sending you out like lambs among wolves."

—Luke 10:2–3 AMP

Then Jesus explained: "My nourishment comes from doing the will of God, who sent me, and from finishing his work. You know the saying, 'Four months between planting and harvest.' But I say, wake up and look around. The fields are already ripe for harvest. The harvesters are paid good wages, and the fruit they harvest is people brought to eternal life. What joy awaits both the planter and the harvester alike!"

—John 4:34–36 NLT

Do your best to present yourself to God as one approved, a worker who has no need to be ashamed, rightly handling the word of truth.

—2 Tim. 2:15 ESV

*Y*ield is one of those words in our English language that have a dual meaning. One meaning is "to give way." The other interpretation is "to produce." Both definitions are applicable to our relationship with God. God is planting and watering a crop that will yield a harvest for us to work, and when we yield to His ways, we will reap a reward.

God is such an awesome God. He does not need us for anything, yet He includes us in His purpose and His sovereign will. As such, He instructs us to yield to His command to go and make disciples in His name. He sets us up for success when He places us in situations where we can tell of all His wonderful deeds. When talking about how God saved and transformed us, God will draw others to salvation and into a deeper relationship with Christ. Making people aware of what God does will at times plant seeds of salvation in someone's heart. Sometimes seeds planted by another are watered, and sometimes a harvest is accomplished when someone becomes a Christian.

We yield to God's command to talk about Him and what He has done for us because it will ultimately yield a harvest of believers. The first and most important story we tell is the account of Christ's salvation. God loves us so much that He had His only Son come to earth as a man. As a man, Jesus was to reverse the curse on humanity after Adam and Eve sinned. Jesus took all the sins and curses of mankind onto Himself. He died a horrific, painful death and became separated from His Father before He rose from the grave three days later. Consequently, the blood Jesus shed and the love He has for us covers a multitude of sins when we believe this and confess Jesus as our Lord and Savior.

The second story we get to share is the story of what God did and does for us individually. He saved us from spiritual death, healed our brokenness, and provided for all our needs, along with many other things. God produces a yield for harvesting when we talk about Him to others.

I am grateful for a God who Yields a harvest and requires us to Yield to His ways as we partner with Him in His kingdom's glory. I once heard, "God's ecosystem is the only one where you plant in someone else's garden and yield a harvest in your own." When we surrender to God and His instruction to make disciples, we reap all kinds of rewards and blessings. That's how awesome our God is. He is a God who says we are to bless others but then turns around and blesses us exponentially in return. The harvest is ripe. Who among you are willing to go? "Here I am. Send me!" (Isa. 6:8).

Recommended worship:
"Here I Am, Lord" by Dan Schutte

Z – Zealous

For the Lord your God is a consuming fire; He is a jealous (impassioned) God [demanding what is rightfully and uniquely His].

—Deut. 4:24 AMP

I have loved you, my people, with an everlasting love. With unfailing love I have drawn you to myself.

—Jer. 31:3 NLT

The Lord your God is in your midst, a victorious warrior. He will exult over you with joy, He will be quiet in His love, He will rejoice over you with shouts of joy.

—Zeph. 3:17 NASB 1995

There are some words that just don't seem to get used as frequently as they used to in years past. I think *zealous* is one of those words. It is possible that some of our younger generation don't even know what the word means. We can define it as "a focused desire, characterized by passion and commitment."

I love sports, especially football. There was a time when

I was a fanatic, a zealot. Football was my allegiance and my life. Every one of my relationships (the few I managed to have) knew it. I gave football priority over people; I passionately pursued it at all costs. I talked it, I breathed it, and I was consumed by sports. It was my addiction. I watched it every day of the week, even recording games to get my "fix" whenever I needed it.

God has this same zeal but a thousand times more. Like a consuming fire, His burning passion is aimed at you. He will pursue you, moving everything and everyone out of the way to make you His child and spend time with you. His love is insatiable, and He literally went to hell in pursuit of you. Have you ever known anyone who loves you so much that they pursued you at all costs, even death, if necessary? We tell our loved ones we love them enough to die for them, but would we really? The Bible says, "Greater love has no one than this: to lay down one's life for one's friends" (John 15:13). While there may be some other examples, I've only known one to actually do it, and His name is Jesus.

In the Bible, God's zeal is often characterized as jealousy. He is a jealous God but is righteous in His jealousy. God created you for Himself. He loves you so much just the way you are, yet He is jealous when you pursue Satan. Anything that is opposed to God's character or placed in a priority position over God is a pursuit of the wrong god, Satan. For me, that was football, but my best friend soon took over that role when I released my grip on football. My zealous God chased me down. He never stopped until I surrendered football and my friend, and I became zealous for my Lord.

Some would say I'm a Jesus freak now, but I wear the label with pride.

I am grateful for a Zealous God who did not give up on me even though I put things and people ahead of Him. His righteous jealousy manifested in His fervent pursuit of me until He had my heart, soul, and mind. Now I am His daughter and friend. I would die for Him if that were what He chose for me.

Recommended worship:
"Insatiable" by Kim Walker-Smith;
"All-Consuming Fire" by Leeland

Acknowledgments

I want to take a few moments to say thank you. First, I want to thank God my Father and my Lord and Savior Jesus Christ for giving me the opportunity through writing to glorify Him. I am only now beginning to have an understanding of who God really is and His character. These 26 days have opened my eyes to see Him better. I thank the Holy Spirit for inspiring these devotionals and teaching me to trust in His faithfulness. Nearly every day I woke up without knowing what I would write. Many of those days I didn't even have a word, or the Holy Spirit changed what I was going to use that morning. Everything in these devotions He AUTHORed as I sat down and wrote.

These 26 days opened a DOOR that showed me how BEAUTIFUL it is to EMPTY myself of pride and embrace the INTIMACY I receive in His FORGIVENESS. His LIGHT continues to illuminate areas that require His GRACE. He is a JUST God, yet my MEDIATOR, Jesus, took my punishment and thereby closed the gap God used to PURSUE me. He is all I need; there is nothing in any QUANTITY that will ever come close to what I have in Christ. Over the past year, He has been my COMFORTER as He HEALED me and taught me to abide in His VINE. Our God is OMNIPRESENT, OMNISCIENT, and OMNIPOTENT, and yet, He KNOWS us individually. He is ZEALOUS for us to YIELD and be NEAR to Him. My UNCHANGING God chased me down and TRANSFORMED me, EXHORTING me each step of my WALK with Him. He SHEPHERDS me to REST in Him. I am grateful and EXALT His holy name.

I would also like to thank Megan. She provided her knowledge and wisdom throughout the entire process, and these devotionals are much better because of it. Megan reminded me of things from our walk that helped give examples of God's character. When I didn't know what word to use, she came up with excellent ones like *Knowing*, *Yielding*, and *Unchanging*, and she helped guide me in the right direction when I had writer's block. She was a constant encouragement, and every day she faithfully gave me positive feedback, even on days when I didn't like how it turned out. She painstakingly edited each devotional and drew all the illustrations. Thank you, Megan, for partnering with me in the kingdom of heaven's work.

I also want to give a big thank you to Norma Jean. Her persistent encouragement led to the book you have in your hands. Without her, the devotionals I wrote would simply be a passing memory to a few friends and family. Thank you for believing these devotionals are meant for a larger audience.

Lastly, I would like to thank my friends and family for their support and encouragement. All the likes, hearts, and personal notes on social media encouraged me. I set out to bless my circle with these devotionals and instead received many blessings of my own.